Color Their Wo

The Art of Creating Strong Customer Loyalty

Activity and Coloring Book

It takes a certain something extra to build lasting customer relationships and handle challenging service situations with care. That's why I created this book — to give you a creative outlet that lets you relax, unwind and own the many ways you make a difference to your customers and the people you work with every day. Just as a painter's palette is filled with many different colors, there are many ways to brighten up a customer's grey mood. And, like an artist, you can color their world with positive experiences. On each page of this book you'll find a sentence starter to reflect on as you set your imagination free by coloring the whimsical images. Use the pages at the back of the book to capture your thoughts. The creative process sets you up for success by lowering stress, raising resilience, and sparking ideas to solve your most pressing customer care problems. Enjoy each page personally or use it with your team. (It's uplifting and sometimes surprising to hear what your peers think and do!) Enjoy yourself and keep inspired as you turn your customer care into an art form.

By
Marilyn Suttle
Keynote Speaker, Coach and Bestselling Author
www.MarilynSuttle.com

Suttle Enterprises LLC
Personal and Professional Growth Training
Suttle Shifts for Big Breakthroughs at Work and in Life

To order customized copies, contact info@MarilynSuttle.com or phone 248.348.1023.

This book
belongs to:

_____

One way
I stay calm
under pressure
is ...

The tone

of my

voice

has the power to ...

One of the best things I say to calm an upset customer is ...

Being patient with customers helps me to ...

A
great way
I handle
customer complaints is ...

The nicest compliment a customer ever gave me was...

A time
I supported
a team member
was ...

One thing
I learned
NOT to say
to
customers
is...

One idea
I have to
improve
customer
service
is ...

If my best customers described me they'd likely say...

Things that turn me into a loyal customer are ...

A little something extra I do to make customers happy is ...

The most rewarding thing about my work is...

Someone who inspires me to do my best is ...

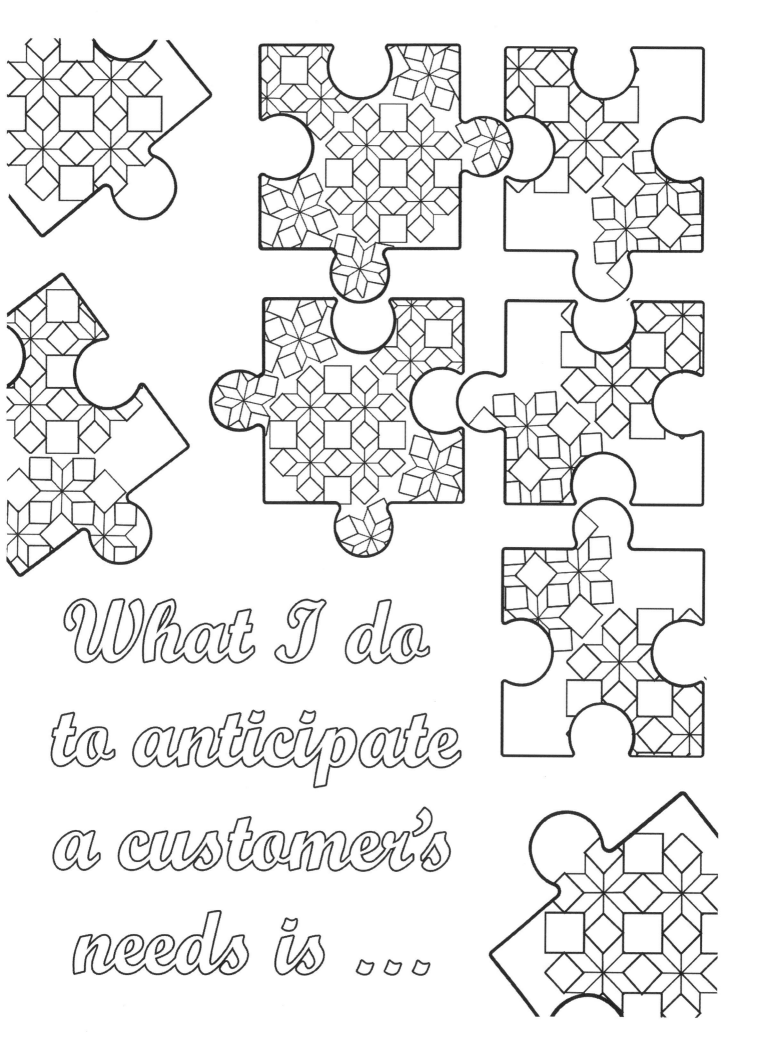

What I do
to anticipate
a customer's
needs is ...

CAPTURE YOUR THOUGHTS

1. One way I stay calm under pressure is _____
   _____
   _____
   _____
   _____

2. I make a good first impression by _____
   _____
   _____
   _____
   _____

3. The tone of my voice has the power to _____
   _____
   _____
   _____
   _____

4. One of the best things I say to calm an upset customer is _____
   _____
   _____
   _____
   _____

5. Being patient with customers helps me to _____
   _____
   _____
   _____
   _____

6. To make my written communication friendly and effective I _____
   _____
   _____
   _____
   _____

7. When I'm preparing for a challenging conversation I _____
   _____
   _____
   _____
   _____

CAPTURE YOUR THOUGHTS

8. A great way I handle customer complaints is _____
_____
_____
_____
_____

9. The best customer service advice I ever got was _____
_____
_____
_____
_____

10. The nicest compliment a customer ever gave me was _____
_____
_____
_____
_____

11. A time I supported a team member was _____
_____
_____
_____
_____

12. I feel most supported by my team when _____
_____
_____
_____
_____

13. One thing I learned NOT to say to customers is _____
_____
_____
_____
_____

14 One idea I have to improve customer service is _____
_____
_____
_____
_____

CAPTURE YOUR THOUGHTS

15. If my best customers described me they'd likely say _____

_____

_____

_____

_____

16. If my coworkers described me they'd probably say _____

_____

_____

_____

_____

17. What I want to be known for is _____

_____

_____

_____

_____

18. Things that turn me into a loyal customer are _____

_____

_____

_____

_____

19. A little something extra I do to make customers happy is _____

_____

_____

_____

_____

20. The most rewarding thing about my work is _____

_____

_____

_____

_____

21. When I need to say "No" I remember to _____

_____

_____

_____

_____

CAPTURE YOUR THOUGHTS

22. One area I'd like more training in is _____
   _____
   _____
   _____
   _____

23. Someone who inspires me to do my best is _____
   _____
   _____
   _____
   _____

24. What I do to anticipate a customer's needs is _____
   _____
   _____
   _____
   _____

25. What I appreciate most about myself is _____
   _____
   _____
   _____
   _____

WANT MORE RESOURCES TO SUPPORT YOUR SUCCESS?

Download the FREE instruction guide:

Use the **COLOR THEIR WORLD** activity book for training and reinforcing ways to create strong customer loyalty. Get the Instruction Guide now at: **www.MarilynSuttle.com/colortheirworld**

Read these books:

Who's Your Gladys? How to Turn Even the Most Difficult Customer Into Your Biggest Fan

Taming Gladys! The Busy Leader's Guide to Creating Fierce Customer Loyalty

Take this training:

The Customer Service Road Map is a course that trains employees so they can form connected, positive relationships with even the most challenging customers. It's done in bite-sized segments over time — as a self-guided study or in facilitated sessions — and can be achieved in one of three ways.

1. We can provide the LMS with an online portal.
2. Use your internal LMS.
3. Get the DVD set with instructor's guide.

Our first-year customer average ROI is 420%! For details and to watch a free module, visit: www.CustomerServiceRoadmap.com or call 248.348.1023.

Request a Keynote, Training and Group or Individual Coaching:

Marilyn Suttle
CEO of Suttle Enterprises LLC
Email: Marilyn@MarilynSuttle.com | Phone: (248) 348.1023 | www.MarilynSuttle.com

Find Marilyn on Twitter: @MarilynSuttle | LinkedIn: www.linkedin.com/in/marilynsuttle

About The Author:

Marilyn Suttle is an inspirational customer service speaker, human potential coach, and best-selling author based out of Metro-Detroit. She works with leaders and teams that want to attract and retain customers, inspire employee engagement and create strong connected relationships. For 20 years she has trained thousands on relationship-strengthening communication and success strategies. Her clients have won industry awards, raised customer satisfaction levels and gotten lasting results in reducing stress and experiencing greater success and self-fulfillment. She's also a social media pro, humanizing the online connection. Marilyn's advice has been featured on TV news, and media like U.S. News and World Report, Ladies Home Journal, and Inc. to name a few.

24351242R00037

Made in the USA
Columbia, SC
22 August 2018